Time for PHONICS

4

Marion Ireland

APPLYING PHONICS IN READING AND SPELLING

HUNTER
EDUCATION
NIGHTINGALE

Published by:
Hunter Education Nightingale
ABN: 69 055 798 626
PO Box 547
Warners Bay NSW 2282
Ph: 0417 658 777
email: sales@huntereducationnightingale.com.au
        paul@huntereducationnightingale.com.au
        www.huntereducationnightingale.com.au

Cover Design: Brooke Lewis

National Library of Australia Card No.
and ISBN 978 - 1 - 925787 - 07 - 8
Phonics Series ISBN 978 - 1 - 925787 - 08 - 5

RECYCLING

When the program is completed and the paper no longer wanted, be sure to have it recycled. The time and care taken to recycle may help save a tree and maintain our environment.

About this Book - *and how to get the best out of it.*

- **Directions** in smaller print give students a clear understanding of what they need to do to get the best outcomes.

This book encompasses a range of strategies including:

- A **phonic approach** using oral phonemic awareness strategies (80% of words in the English language have a phonic base)
- **Word families** consisting of rhyming words. This base list can be expanded as relevant.
- **Varied, graded activities** that are age appropriate.
- **Core words** - simple common sight words that are also high frequency words essential to all reading matter.
- **Word building** - strategies to build understanding and confidence
- **Blends** - consonant blends and special blends are included as they form an essential part of many word families.
- **Syllables** - how to use syllables to decipher new words.
- **Spelling rules** - some basic spelling rules using vocabulary that is relevant to word families at this level.

- **Phonic irregularities** - eg when 'c' has an 's' sound in words like 'city' ; words that look similar but don't rhyme eg has/was ; some words do not look alike yet they rhyme eg said/bed
- **Graded sentences** can form the basis for Dictation and show correct usage of list words. These can be modified as needed.
- **Sentence construction** - students are encouraged to complete and create some of their own oral and written sentences.
- **Compound words** - 'making and breaking' compound words using known words selected from word families
- **Homographs and homophones** - using vocabulary that is common usage and in their word families.
- **Some challenge activities** are incorporated in the mix.
- **Personal Word Box** - words chosen by student and/or teacher, based on student needs. These need to be achievable for individual students.
- **Revision** is built into the sequence of activities.
- **Assessment tasks** measure progress and can also be used as a diagnostic tool.

Message to Parents

With *Time for Phonics Book 4* you may need and want to help your child with some of the word families introduced to make more complex words. As a parent you can work with your child to ensure the basic fundamentals of learning to read with Phonics. Follow the suggested approach with each sound, blend and sentence and as your child's understanding and competence grows reading skills will grow too.

As your child works through the book your help may be required less. However, ensure your child fully understands the process and outcomes of a phonetic approach to reading. Good spelling and writing will follow.

Praise your child at all times, because you are the ideal support person in your child's life to help with developing a good education. It is essential that your child learns to read and spell. *Time for Phonics 4* will provide a brick in the foundations of learning to read. Work with your child, make the learning process fun and enjoy the journey to becoming a good reader.

ay word family

a and y makes its own special sound when you put these letters together to form ay. Put a ring around the ay words in these boxes. Read and spell them aloud.

bay	hill
tray	stay
why	way

day	away
today	pay
pray	dry

Be a detective.

Look for phonic clues.

clay	many
daytime	
play	may

away	prey
try	say
anyway	ray

stray	hay
yesterday	
by	holiday

playtime	lay
birthday	
always	fly

Look for phonic clues. Copy these words and spell them aloud to help you remember them.

they   good   please   because

_____   _____   _____   _____

Put these words together to form compound words. Write neatly and spell them aloud.

Add *ing* to these **ay** words. Write neatly and spell them aloud.

may + be = _____

say + ing = _____

pay + day = _____

stay + ing = _____

run + way = _____

lay + ing = _____

hay + stack = _____

play + ing = _____

Read and spell.

Please put all of your toys away on this tray today. Then you may go and play.

Today we had some good green and blue clay to play with at school. The children will soon be going away for a holiday.

Yesterday the children went out to play at my birthday party because they are always good. They had to stay away from water birds nesting in the bay.

Personal Words

word puzzle - **days of the week**

s		b	e	d	t	i	m	e	s		T		h	i	t
p	i	e		a	i	r	e	l	e	p	h	a	n	t	s
a		m	a	r	c	h		f	l		u		o		h
c	r	a	c	k	k		W	i	l	F	r	i	d	a	y
e		n	e	s	t	s	e	n	d		s	m	i	l	e
s	a	d		M	o	n	d	a	y		d	o	l	l	s
h		o	n	e		o	n	c	e		a	b	o	u	t
i	n	t	o		T	u	e	s	d	a	y		d		o
p	l	a	n	t		n	s	c	r	e	w	s	h	o	p
s	u	n	l	S	u	n	d	a	y			s	h	e	e	p
		u	y	i	s	t	a	m	p	e	r	i	l	w	e
S	a	t	u	r	d	a	y		s	k	i	p	p	e	d

The seven days of the week are all hidden in this puzzle. They all end with day. Circle each one. How many more words can you find in this puzzle?

The two weekend days are _____

and _____. The five school days are

_____

_____

I like _____ day best because

_____.

Rule: When a middle vowel is followed by a consonant and has *e* at the end, the middle vowel has a long sound. The *e* at the end is sometimes called '*magic e*'.

For example, *mat*   becomes   *mate*

short vowel sound   long vowel sound with '*magic e*' at the end

Copy these words and add *e*. The first one is done for you. Read and spell them aloud.

hid   hide   rat   _____

hop   _____   kit   _____

bit   _____   spin   _____

not   _____   shin   _____

mad   _____   mat   _____

car   _____   cut   _____

How many more *a_e* words can you find to write in this box?

Personal Words

ace word family

When you put **a**, **c** and **e** together, **ace** forms its own special sound.
'*Magic e*' at the end gives the letter **a** a long sound and the **c** sounds likes **s**.
Make **ace** words using these beginning sounds. Write them neatly. Read and spell each word aloud.

f   l   r   p   br   pl   tr   sp

_____

_____

Write **ace** in these words then join the words to match the pictures.

a horse r_____

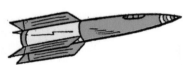

purple l_____s

a funny f_____

a sp_____ ship

Copy these words and spell them aloud to help you remember them.

first   second   third   fourth

_____   _____   _____   _____

In a deck of cards the *ace* has the highest value. Label these cards.

__ __ __   __ __ __   __ __ __   __ __ __

of hearts   of diamonds   of spades   of clubs

Look up the dictionary meaning of the word *ace*, using a book or computer.

Read and spell.

We like to have races at school. I can run at a very fast pace until my face is red.

One day we may be able to race to the stars and planets far out in space. Who will be first to do that?

I wish to travel in a spaceship that can go at a very fast pace. Computers can help bring me back from space to a safe place at home.

Personal Words

Make **ade** words using these beginning single sounds and blends.
Read and spell them aloud.

f   j   m   w   gr   sp   sh   tr   bl   gl

_____

_____

Label the pictures with **ade** words.

a _____

I like to

_____ .

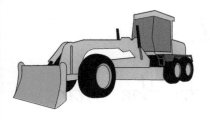

a _____ r

I sit in the

_____ .

a _____

of grass

I _____

my bed.

Use phonic clues for these words ending with **y**. Write them neatly.
Read and spell them aloud.

busy   very   every   only

_____   _____   _____   _____

Tick the sentence that matches the picture.

I made a toy bird.

I sat in the shade.

I made my bed.

Look at the grader.

Look at the parade.

Look at the green jade.

Add *d* to these words and copy them. Read them aloud. Use the sounds to spell them aloud.

fade__ _____   shade__ _____

Read and spell.

When we are busy playing in the shade we only dig with a small spade.

On Friday we played outside in the shade. We made a cubby with some friends. We saw a yellow grader picking up rocks outside.

That very busy man in the faded orange top was about to get onto his grader. He will soon be fixing the street outside the store where they trade in winter.

Personal Words

age word family

Make *age* words using these beginning sounds. The letter *a* says its own name with '*magic e*' at the end. The *g* sounds like *j* in these words. Write them neatly. Read and spell them aloud.

c   p   r   w   s   st

_____

_____

Write *age* in these words. Read and spell them.

man_____   post_____

True or false?

You can put a whale in a cage.   _____

You can turn the pages of a book.   _____

You can tell me your age.   _____

You have been on stage.   _____

Some words end with *al*. Use phonic clues for these words. Copy them neatly. Read and spell them aloud.

person   personal   animal   mammal

_____   _____   _____   _____

Find another word that means *rage*.
Use your dictionary or computer. _____

Word building. Put these syllables together. Write them neatly.
Read and spell them aloud.

in+ter+est+ing= _____ an+i+mal= _____

diff+er+ent= _____ per+son+al= _____

Read and spell.

I turned the pages of my book at school. I like reading about animals.

Some animals are kept in cages where a person can look after them in places like a zoo. Other animals can do tricks on stage.

We looked at animals in cages and felt safe because some can get into a rage. I have a good book with many very interesting pages about different mammals.

Personal Words

Make **ake** words using these single sounds. Write them neatly then read and spell them aloud.

b   c   f   h   l   m   r   s   t   w

_____

_____

Now make more **ake** words using these blends at the beginning.

sh   st   br   dr   fl

_____

Draw a ring around the **ake** words in this box.

back	bake	wake		
stick	take	snake	brake	brick
awake	shake	clock	lake	milkshake
shack	baker	baked	brakes	

Each of these words has a long *i* sound and ends with '*magic e*'. Look for phonic clues. Copy each rhyming word neatly. Read and spell these words aloud.

fire   wire   hire   tire

_____   _____   _____   _____

Add *ing* to these words, then copy them.

camp_____ _____

sleep_____ _____

look_____ _____

Add *ed* to these words, then copy them.

play____ _____

stay____ _____

holiday____ _____

Read and spell.

Can you please bake a cake for me to take home after school?

Our family likes to go camping beside the blue lake in summer. We keep a lookout for snakes because we need to be safe.

Our family and friends went camping beside the blue lake. We had to make our beds before it got dark. We stayed awake until the stars came out because we were not sleepy.

Personal Words

Make **ale** words using these beginning sounds. Write them neatly then read and spell them aloud.

s   p   b   m   sh   st   wh

_____

_____

a book of fairy_____ on my desk

a _____ of hay in the paddock

a _____ blue and white jug

a FOR _____ sign on a car

These words all have the short vowel **u** and they end with **ch**.
Which words rhyme?

such   much   lunch   bunch

_____ _____ _____ _____

Tick the sentences that match each picture:

Whales live on land.

Whales live in deep water.

Whales live on the beach.

These farm animals have a bale of hay.

These farm animals are for sale.

These farm animals have stale bread.

Read and spell.

How big is a whale? It is as big as a long bus or a very big truck.

Have you ever seen a whale? Whales are such big mammals and they are free. We must look after them. They are not for sale.

Whales are mammals. They stay in deep water and swim underwater for a long time. That baby whale is a male calf. It is much smaller swimming next to its mother.

Personal Words

ame word family

Make **ame** words using these beginning sounds. Write them neatly.
Read and spell them aloud.

c   d   f   g   l   s   t   bl   fl   fr

_____

_____

_____

Circle the **ame** words in each row.

| came | come | some | same |

| shame | lame | tame | seem |

| ram | flame | blame | ashamed |

| frame | framed | blamed | tamed |

Circle **any** in these words. The beginning **a** sounds like short **e**.
These are sight words.

any   many   anyway   anyone

_____   _____   _____   _____

True or false?

 A lion is a tame animal. _____

Fire has red and orange flames. _____

 Children like to play games. _____

Read and spell.

We like to play the same games any day after school. That is so much fun.

Many children in our street play the same games before lunch every week. They all have a lot of fun playing and anyone can come.

Many of our friends came to stay for more than a week. We all played the same old games until sundown. We also did some art and made some frames as well.

Personal Words

ane word family

Make **ane** words using these beginning sounds. Write them neatly then read and spell them aloud.

c   D   l   m   p   w   cr   pl

_____

_____

Label these pictures with **ane** words.

a horse with a

_____

a _____
of glass

a red and blue

_____

a yellow

_____

After a full moon, the moon begins to

_____.

Use phonic clues for these words. Write them neatly.
Read and spell them aloud.

visit   visitor   people   once

_____ _____ _____ _____

Some words are exactly the same but have more than one meaning. They are called **homographs**.

crane

I craned my neck like the crane with a long neck to see the top of the very tall crane that was lifting something onto a big ship.

Read and spell.

The silver plane went up into the sky until it seemed small when we looked up.

Our friend went to visit her grandmother and grandfather who lived down a very long lane. She went in a silver plane with lots of other people.

Many different people went in a silver plane for a holiday. Once the plane had lifted them up into the sky, they saw planes and cranes that looked like toys and visitors that looked as small as ants.

Personal Words

Make **ate** words using these beginning sounds. Write them neatly. Read and spell them aloud.

d   f   h   l   m   r   cr   gr   pl   sk   st

_____

_____

_____

_____

What is the date today?

_____

What is the name of your state?

_____

The **u** sound in bull, full and pull sounds like **oo** as in book. The **g** in *large* sounds like *j*.

bull   full   pull   large

_____   _____   _____   _____

Add **s** to these words.

date___   mate___   plate___   crate___

Add **es** to these words.

bus____   gas____   class____   pass____

More homographs

date

Read and spell.

I have a plate of yummy dates and a drink for a snack with my mates.

The children went out to skate at the park with some mates. It was late in the day so they did not stay too late.

'Please shut the gate at the grate,' called dad as he parked his large truck by the shed. He took six crates full of plates from the back and stacked them next to a wall.

Personal Words

Make *ave* words using these beginning sounds. Write them neatly.
Read and spell them aloud.

| c | w | D | p | s | sh | br | cr |

_____

_____

Circle the *ave* word that looks like the other words but it does **not** rhyme with any of them.

| pave | save | slave | brave | cave |
| shave | have | Dave | crave | grave |

Now look at these words and think about them.

go+es = goes rhymes with *toes* ;

do+es = does rhymes with *buzz*

said rhymes with *bed*; *was* rhymes with *Ros*;

gone rhymes with *scone*

Some words are just a bit tricky!

These are all sight words but you can still use phonic clues. Copy them neatly. Read and spell them aloud.

goes   does   said   gone

_____   _____   _____   _____

Break these compound words into two separate words.

caveman = _____ + _____

playmate = _____ + _____

milkshake = _____ + _____

underwater = _____ + _____

sometimes = _____ + _____

Read and spell.

One brave girl said that she had gone into a cave by the sea with her friend, Ros.

Have you ever gone into a cave? Dave said that you have to be brave because sometimes a big wave does go inside caves by the sea.

Many people save postage stamps. They put them in an album or a stock book and only let best friends look at them. Brave Dave said that he does still save some stamps. It is his hobby.

Personal Words

adding **ing**

Rule: Words like these that end with an *e* drop the final *e* before adding *ing*. Write the missing words on this grid. Cross out the final *e* in the middle row. The first one is done for you.

come	come	coming
have	_____	having
race	race	_____
give	_____	_____
live	_____	living
wade	_____	_____
hide	hide	_____
ride	_____	riding
excite	_____	_____
skate	_____	_____
smile	smile	_____
snore	_____	_____
paddle	_____	_____
sizzle	_____	sizzling

word puzzle - words ending in **ing**

Use a coloured pencil to circle words ending with *ing*.
There are 21 in this puzzle.

t	h	e	g	s	m	i	l	i	n	g
h			i	t	s		i	l	o	o
i	h	a	v	i	n	g	o	i	t	i
n		r	i	n	o	w	n	v	e	n
g		t	n	g	r	a	c	i	n	g
w	i	n	g		i		o	n	b	m
d	o	i	n	g	n	o	m	g	e	a
r	i	d	i	n	g		i	s	i	k
o	h	o	p	i	n	g	n	i	n	i
s	i	z	z	l	i	n	g	n	g	n
e	p	a	d	d	l	i	n	g		g

(21 words ending with ing are either horizontal or vertical. Some letters overlap. The answers are in alphabetical order here: being coming doing giving going gracing having hoping living making paddling racing riding ring sing smiling sizzling snoring sting thing wing)

27

Some words like these have the letter **c** that sounds like **s**. Copy them neatly. Read and spell them aloud.

cents _____   centre _____

cylinder _____   city _____

prince _____   princess _____

Words like **centimetre** and **excited** also have a **c** that sounds like **s**. Copy neatly.

centimetre _____   exciting _____

Only the beginning **c** sound in **circle** and **circus** sounds like **s**.

circle _____

circus _____

Write a sentence about a circus.

_____

_____

_____

Put these syllables together and write the words.

des+ert = _____   cent+i+metre = _____

a+cross = _____   prin+cess = _____

ex+cur+sion = _____   cir+cle = _____

ex+cite+ment = _____   cir+cus = _____

Read and spell.

Some children from the city went by bus to see small animals hiding and living in the desert.

Some people from the city went on an exciting trip to a desert. They saw animals hiding behind rocks, living on land with not much water.

Some people from the city went on an exciting excursion to the centre of a desert. They saw small animals living under rocks, hiding from the hot sun and coming out after dark to find food.

Personal Words

'*Magic e*' at the end of these words gives the vowel *i* a long sound.
Make *ice* words using these beginning sounds. Write them neatly.
Read and spell them aloud.

d   l   m   n   r   sl   sp   pr

_____

_____

True or false?

A dice has numbers 1-6. _____

Mice like cheese. _____

An iceberg is made of ice. _____

Icebergs never melt. _____

Fish live in cold water under the ice. _____

These words all have **ere** at the end but only some of them rhyme!
Read and spell them.

here   were   where   there

_____ _____ _____ _____

Look at the sentences below. Finish writing the words that have these blends.

sl_____   pl_____   dr_____   wh____

wh_____   wh_____   th___   ___th   th____

th___   th_____   th_____   _____th _____

Read and spell.

We all had a nice slice of birthday
cake and a drink with ice at the party.

The drinks were cold with ice. We gave Dave a
slice of cake and he said, 'Thank you. I am glad
you had such a nice day.'

There are some nice places where mammals live in
white snow. The sea is so cold that the top turns
to ice. They were busy hunting and fishing when
the icebergs began to melt.

Personal Words

'*Magic e*' at the end of these words gives the vowel *i* a long sound.
Make *ide* words using these beginning sounds. Write them neatly.
Read and spell them aloud.

h   r   s   t   w   gl   sl   br   pr

_____

_____

Put these words together to make compound words.

hide+out= _____   be+side= _____

in+side= _____   out+side= _____

Copy these words and add *r*. Read and spell them aloud.

ride _____   wide _____

glide _____

walk and **talk** are sight words.
Copy these words neatly.

Look at the middle vowel with *e* at the end. Copy these words neatly.

walk   talk   these   those

_____   _____   _____   _____

True or false?

A spider can spin a web made of silk. _____

The tide comes in and goes out at the seaside. _____

We can ride on the back of a unicorn. _____

Some animals can talk. _____

Many people like to ride bikes. _____

Read and spell.

We like to play hide and seek. It is fun to ride a bike to my place.

'Just look at those black spiders on the wall outside,' said Fred. 'They are upside down in a web of silk. They hide when we walk by.'

Yesterday we played hide and seek. These friends walked inside and outside until they saw me beside the hideout. After, we all went for a bike ride down a wide lane.

Personal Words

'*Magic e*' at the end of these words gives the vowel *i* a long sound. Make **ile** words using these beginning sounds. Write them neatly. Read and spell them aloud.

f   m   p   t   sm   st   wh

_____

_____

Copy these words and add *d*. Read and spell them aloud.

use _____   pile _____

smile _____

Write the missing words in this sentence. (*use*   *used*   *wanted*)

Both men _____ a spade to shift

sand they _____ to _____

at another place.

Use phonic clues for these sight words. Copy them neatly. Read and spell them aloud.

use   both   want   picture

_____   _____   _____   _____

Tick the sentence that matches the picture.

Many people are wading while it is sunny.

Some children are making piles of sand.

Many people are smiling at the dark sky.

The word *file* is a **homograph** with more than one meaning.

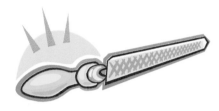 file

Read and spell.

A pile of bricks was lifted from the back of a truck and put next to the tiles.

My best friend smiles when she is happy. She looked at me while I told her a funny story then we both smiled at the ending.

We like our best friends to give us happy smiles. Sometimes they do that while we are both talking and walking on brown tiles on our way to the city centre to see a picture.

Personal Words

'*Magic e*' at the end of these words gives the vowel *i* a long sound. Make *ine* words using these beginning sounds. Write them neatly. Read and spell them aloud.

$$d \quad f \quad l \quad m \quad n \quad p \quad v \quad w \quad sp \quad sh$$

_____

_____

Write *nine* then add *ty* to make the word for 90. _____

Break these compound words into two separate words.

underline = _____ + _____

sunshine = _____ + _____

cartwheels = _____ + _____

These are sight words. Use phonic clues to help you read them. Write them neatly. Read and spell them aloud.

work   world   done   also

_____   _____   _____   _____

Break these words into syllables. Read and spell them aloud.

internet = ____ + _____ + _____   present = _____ + _____

lemon = _____ + ____   enjoy = ____ + _____

strong = _____ + _____   relax = ____ + _____

relaxing = ____ + _____ + _____

Read and spell.

One fine day nine old men took some fishing lines to the creek to fish.

Fishing is relaxing so nine people sat under pine trees by the water. When a man felt a strong tug on his line, he wanted to pull in a large fish.

Fish is fine when it is cooked over a campfire using pine logs that burn well. You want a large, strong frying pan with butter sizzling to cook nine fish. I also enjoy mine with lemon.

Personal Words

ind word family

i also has a long sound in this word family. Make *ind* words using these beginning sounds. Write them neatly. Read and spell them aloud.

b   f   h   k   m   r   w   gr

_____

_____

_____

Word building.

bind+er= _____   kind+ness= _____

kind+ly= _____   un+kind= _____

re+mind= _____   re+mind+er= _____

re+mind+ing= _____   re+mind+ed= _____

un+wind= _____   re+wind= _____

was is a tricky sight word. *on* in the next three words sounds like *un*

was   won   wonder   wonderful

_____ _____ _____ _____

one and *won* are homophones. They sound the same but they each have different spelling and different meaning. Write *one* or *won* in these sentences.

On sports day I _____ a race. I came first.

I _____ a game at my friend's party.

_____ is a small number.

Read and spell.

Do you ever find
That some people
Are not very kind?

Do you ever find
That some people
Just wind you up?

Never mind,
You can still be kind
And find a way to be
The kindest person ever.

Personal Words

Use these beginning sounds to write some *ow* words. They must all rhyme with *cow*.

b   c   h   n   r   s   v   w   br

_____

_____

_____

Use these beginning sounds to make some *ow* words with *n* at the end. The first one is done for you. Write them neatly. Read and spell them aloud.

d   g   t   cl   br   cr   dr   fr

down _____

_____

_____

These are sight words. Use phonic clues. Write them neatly. Read and spell them aloud.

calf   half   ask   watch

_____   _____   _____   _____

Add *er* to these rhyming *ow* words. Read and spell them aloud.

show____   tow____   bow____   flow____   pow____

Write the missing *ow* words to complete these sentences.

A _____ of rain fell on this

pretty sun_____. It has yellow

petals and _____ seeds.

Read and spell.

How are you today? Now you must go down to the town to see the funny clown.

We went all the way to town by car to see a very funny clown doing clever tricks. On the way we saw a brown mother cow with a calf.

People like to watch clowns doing clever tricks when the circus is in town. How do they turn those cartwheels? Some clowns visit sick children who feel good because a clown makes them smile.

Personal Words

Make **ail** words using these beginning sounds. Write them neatly.
Read and spell them aloud.

b   f   h   j   m   n   p   r   t   w   tr   sn

_____

_____

_____

Circle the correct word inside the brackets.

We went shopping because the shops had a (sail/sale).

Men and boys are (mail/male).

At bedtime my sister read a fairy (tale/tail) about Pinocchio and the (wail/whale).

There was a storm and (hale/hail)stones fell to the ground.

A snail left a silver trail near the (bail/bale) of hay.

Use phonic clues to help you read and spell these maths words ending in **ty**. Write them neatly.

twenty   thirty   forty   fifty   sixty

_____ _____ _____ _____ _____

Pair the words in this box to form compound words to match the pictures. Write them neatly.

| way | rail | or | sail | or | mail | tail | man |

_____ _____ _____ _____

Read and spell.

When I am sick or hurt at home I can send an email to my friends at school.

People everywhere like to send emails because it is much quicker than snail mail and you do not even need to use a postage stamp.

When people write emails to family and friends it is quicker than snail mail and you do not need a mailman. Your computer does that. You only need to click the button to send your letter with pictures.

Personal Words

Make **ain** words using these beginning sounds. Write them neatly.
Read and spell them aloud.

g   m   p   r   pl   dr   br   gr   tr   ch   st

_____

_____

Add **ain** to these words and copy them. Read and spell them aloud.

ag_____   _____   ag_____st   _____

Make rhyming words for these.
Read and spell them aloud.

faint   p_____

s_____

Add **ed** to these words.
Read and spell them aloud.

faint____

paint____

Copy each word and add **ing**.

rain   _____

drain   _____

train   _____

gain   _____

chain   _____

More words with double consonants in the middle and **y** at the end.
Copy them neatly. Read and spell them aloud.

carry   marry   curry   hurry

_____   _____   _____

Put these syllables together to make whole words.

won + der + ful = _____   ad + ven + ture = _____

Put these words together to make compound words.

rain + forest = _____   rain + fall = _____

rain + drop = _____   rain + bow = _____

Read and spell.

The family went a long way to town by train. It rained all the way. It just did not stop.

It was raining when they stopped in the city. People from the train were carrying bags and running to get out of the rain. They wanted to stay dry.

Everyone was hurrying here and there. The city was very busy with people, cars and buses, trucks, bikes and trains. Drains were full of running water. When the rain stopped they were all happy to see a pretty rainbow.

Personal Words

Make **air** words using these beginning sounds. Write them neatly.
Read and spell them aloud.

f   h   p   fl   st   ch

_____

Write words to match these pictures.

_ _ _ _ _ _ _   _ _ _ _ _ _ _   _ _ _ _ _ _ _

   a _____      a _____

of socks   of shoes

Homophones sound the same but have different meanings and different
spelling.

   pair      pear

There is only one **l** at the end of words like **colourful**. Read and spell these
words aloud.

colour   colourful   money   buy

_____ _____ _____ _____

money and buy are both sight words. Use phonic clues to help you remember them. Read and spell them aloud.
Write the missing words in these sentences.

I had some _____ to take to town

to____ some toys at the toyshop.

Some were very c_____ful .

Read and spell.

How can you make your fair or dark hair red or yellow or green or purple?

Mum sprayed colour on my fair hair to make it purple and blue because it was Mufti Day at our school. We all had colour in our hair and gave money to help others.

It was fun to sit on chairs on Mufti Day at school and have different colours sprayed onto our hair. One pair of girls with fair hair looked very colourful. We did it to give money to people who need our help.

Personal Words

---

ea word family

Make *ea* words using these beginning sounds. The *ea* in these words sounds like *ee*. Write them neatly. Read and spell them aloud.

p   s   t   fl   _____

Add *t* at the end to make more *ea* words that rhyme with *eat*. Read and spell them aloud.

m   s   b   h   ch   tr   wh

eat _____

_____

ea words ending in *d* have a short *e* sound in words like

bread   tread   instead

Circle the correct word in brackets in each sentence.

Ships sail on the (see/sea).

My dog has (fleas/flees).

I like to eat (meet/meat).

Where have you (been/bean)?

Lots of words end with *ly*. Practise reading and spelling these. Write them neatly.

neatly   really   suddenly   exactly

_____

Write *ea* in these words: one l___f   two l___ves

More *ea* words with a *ee* sound. Write neatly.
Read and spell these words aloud.

jeans   m___l   h___l

r___l   r___lly   s___l   st___l

h___p   l___p   cr___m   dr___m   ch___p

Read and spell.

I have been reading a book about a very green
rainforest with animals that eat a lot of meat.

Rainforests have really tall trees, vines and moss.
There are rocks in creeks. Some go all the way to
the sea where birds and animals find meat to eat.

Many wonderful animals and birds make homes
across rainforests. Some only need meat to eat.
Others live on clean, green plants. There is a lot of
heat and rain where really tall trees give cool shade.

Personal Words

Make **each** words using these beginning sounds. Write them neatly.
Read and spell them aloud.

b   p   r   t

each _____

Add **es** to the words you have just written. The first one is done for you.

beaches _____   _____   _____

teach+ **er** = _____   teach+ **ing** = _____

Tick the sentence that matches the picture.

The family is going to the beach.

The family is eating peaches for tea.

The family is having lunch on the beach.

Dad is teaching us at the beach.

These words are not spelt the way they sound. They are sight words.
Use phonic clues.

love   dove   glove   above

_____   _____   _____

A **palindrome** is a word that is the same when you spell it backwards.
Try writing and spelling these words backwards.

dad _____   noon _____   pop _____

level _____   kayak _____

radar _____   racecar _____

peep _____   wow _____

did _____   pup _____

Read and spell.

Each of the children went to see the teacher about the books that she was marking.

The teacher told each of the children that they are doing very good work. She reached above her chair to get some stickers to give to them.

We loved it when our teacher took us to the beach for an excursion. We paddled in the water above the waves and had races on the sand. We each had ripe peaches and ice-cream with our lunch.

Personal Words

Make **ear** words using these beginning sounds. Write them neatly.
The first one is done for you. Read and spell them aloud.

d   f   h   n   r   t   y   cl   sp   sh

dear _____

_____

Word building. Add *ing* to these words and copy them neatly.

hear_____   _____   clear_____   _____

Add **er** to these words and copy them neatly.

near____   _____   shear____   _____

Add **est** to these words and copy them neatly.

dear_____   _____   clear_____   _____

Add *ly* to these words and copy them neatly.

near____   _____

dear____   _____

Sound these rhyming words. Write them neatly.
Read and spell them aloud.

catch   match   batch   hatch

_____ _____ _____ _____

Write the missing words to match the pictures. (clear ears hear year)

There are 365 days in one _____.

I _____ with my two _____.

The sky was _____ when the plane took off.

Read and spell.

Mother can hear her dear little baby crying.
She will wipe his tears away.

The busy shearer goes to the shearing shed to shear
many sheep. Every year he has to catch one at a
time from each batch in the pens.

Shearing is a busy time on wheat and sheep farms.
The farmer brings the sheep in from the paddock for
shearers to catch them from the pens nearby. It is
clear that the wool has to come off this year.

Personal Words

Use these beginning sounds to make some *ow* words. They must all rhyme with *slow*. Write them neatly. Read and spell each one aloud. The first one is done for you.

b   l   bl   m   r   s   sl   sn   t

fl   gl   gr   sh   st   thr

bow _____

_____

Some words look and sound exactly the same. They are even spelt the same way but have more than one meaning. They are called **homographs**.

   *bow*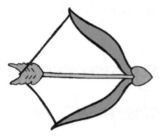

Some words sound the same but are spelt differently and have different meanings. These are called **homophones**.

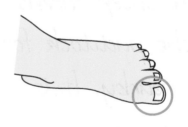   *toe*      *tow*

These words have a long *o* sound with '*magic e*' at the end. Read and spell them aloud.

bone   **drone**   **tone**   **stone**

_____   _____   _____   _____

Write the missing *ow* sound in the words in these sentences. Read and spell them aloud.

From the wind____ I saw a sparr____ in a will____ tree. He had a yell____ beak.

When it is sunny my shad____ seems to foll____ me everywhere I go.

Read and spell.

The children looked out the window at a drone and snow falling in the garden.

The wind had blown some trees down before it began to snow. White snow glowed in the sun. The children were able to throw snowballs at each other.

These children live where it always snows in winter. White snow glowed in the sun so they made snowballs to throw at each other. They stopped to make a snowman near a pile of stones under a willow tree.

Personal Words

adding **es** or **ed**

Rule: Change the *y* to *i* before adding *es* or *ed* in words like these. Write the missing words in these columns. The first one is done for you. Cross out the *y* in the words in Column 2 and write *i* in its place before adding *es* or *ed* in columns 3 and 4. Write neatly. Read and spell them aloud.

COLUMN 1	COLUMN 2	COLUMN 3	COLUMN 4
crying	cry	cries	cried
frying	fry	_____	fried
trying	_____	tries	_____
drying	dry	_____	_____
spying	_____	spies	_____
ferrying	ferry	_____	ferried
partying	_____	parties	_____
hurrying	hurry	_____	_____

Change the *y* to *i* and add *es* to these words. The first one is done for you.

fly	flies	story	_____
puppy	_____	jelly	_____
berry	_____	family	_____

56

word puzzle - **consonant blends**

There are 20 words in this puzzle beginning with these consonant blends

bl cl fl gl pl br dr fr gr pr tr sk sm sn sp st sw

Use coloured pencils to put a circle around each one. The words are all either horizontal or vertical. Some letters overlap.

s	k	a	t	i	n	g	l	o	w	s
w	h	e	r	e		g			p	m
i		y	u	s	s	r	t	s	l	i
m	a	t	s	e	p	o	r	t	a	l
m	a	h	t	f	i	w	o	o	n	e
i	h	e	a	r	d	r	o	n	e	d
n	o	o	n	i	e	a	p	e	a	s
g	l	i	d	e	r	c	l	o	w	n
f	l	o	w	n	b	l	a	m	e	a
b	r	e	a	d	e	d	r	i	n	k
p	r	i	n	c	e	s	s	h	e	e

The answers are in alphabetical order here:

(blame bread clown drink drone flown friend glider glow/glows grow plane princess skating smiled snake spider stand stone troop swim/swimming)

Do not circle any more words but there are also 3 special blends - (she the where) and many other words if you overlap and use some of the same letters more than once. Look for smaller words in some of the bigger words and you will find:

am an and ape awe bee end he hear in ink lane led lid low mat mile noon on one own no pea plan portal read tan tone

Challenge – can you find any more?

oa word family

Use these beginning and end sounds to make some *oa* words. Write them neatly. Read and spell each one aloud. The first one is done for you.

boat   g___t   c___t   m___t   fl__t

c___l   f__l   l_f   l__n   m___n

Put a tick next to the sentence that matches the picture.

A red and blue boat is floating in the air.

This green and white boat is for sale.

A blue and red boat is floating in the bay.

Write a pretend sentence about a baby foal.

_____

_____

_____

_____

Look for blends in three of these words. Use phonic clues to help you with sight words.

wash   fresh   brush   idea   care

_____ _____ _____ _____ _____

Write *ful* at the end of these words. The first one is done for you.

wonder_____   wonderful

play_____   _____

cheer_____   _____

Read and spell.

Baby goats are kids. A goat is a good pet but you must brush its coat and give it some oats.

A pet goat needs clean, fresh water and food. You need to take good care of its coat by brushing it. Goats like to eat oats and other grains but they can eat anything.

Goats will even eat plants that have thorns like blackberries and roses. They like oats and other grains but do not let them eat the washing that is drying on the line. A goat is a playful pet. It is a good idea to brush its coat.

Personal Words

ou word family

Use these beginning and end sounds to make some **ou** words. Write them neatly. Read and spell each one aloud.

___r   ___t   h___r   s___r   l___d

al___d   cl___d   c___nt   m___nt   m___ntain

f___ntain   am___nt   ab___t   b___nd

h___nd   s___nd   r___nd   ar___nd

gr___nd   playgr___nd   merry-go-r___nd

Break these compound words into two separate words.

outback = _____ + _____

playground = _____ + _____

soundproof = _____ + _____

soundtrack = _____ + _____

merry-go-round

Break these words into syllables.

amount = _____   ground = _____

mountain = _____   fountain = _____

Look at short **o** and **ss** in these words. Sound each word. Read and spell them aloud.

boss   **moss**   **possum**   **blossom**

_____ _____ _____ _____

Write the missing words in these sentences.

| playground   merry-go-round   mountain   around |

The kids played in the _____ before

going _____ and _____

on the big _____. Next, they went

for a bike ride up a _____.

Read and spell.

Possums live in the bush. They can hear the
sound of animals and birds all around them
in the trees and on the ground.

A mother possum is looking out of her tree hollow. She
can hear the many different sounds of other animals and
birds all around her in the tall trees and on the ground.

A family of possums lives on a mountain where they
found a hollow with dry moss. They hear many different
sounds made by other animals and birds all around them
in the trees and on the ground as they feed on blossoms
and berries.

Personal Words

Assessment Tasks

Circle the correct words in these sentences.

1. A rose is a (flour / flower).

2. A horse has a (mane / main).

3. I can (here / hear) the bell ringing.

4. The postman brings our (mail / male).

Mark / 4

Pair words in this box to form six compound words. Write them on the lines.

rain	friend	ball	down
ground	every	play	forest
snow	where	stairs	ship

_____

_____

_____

Mark / 6

Assessment Task

Teacher direction: Say each word once. Read the sentence. Repeat the word.

1. **away**   I am going away for a holiday.

2. **shine**   The sun will shine today.

3. **space**   Astronauts travel through space.

4. **shade**   When it is hot we sit in the shade.

5. **stage**   Actors perform on stage.

6. **because** I will go inside because it is raining.

7. **animals** Some animals live on farms.

8. **take**   I will take my book to the library.

9. **every**   I go to sleep every night.

10. **whale**   A whale swims in the ocean.

11. **came**   My friend came home with me.

12. **such**   We need to rest on such a hot day.

13. **plane**   A pilot flies the plane.

14. **people**   People like to visit the zoo.

15. **many**   There are too many cars.

16. **plate**   I have fish and chips on my plate.

17. **large**   A large truck stopped at the lights.

18. **said**   We said 'hello' to our visitor.

19. **does**   Jim likes ice-cream. So does Pam.

20. **underwater** I can swim underwater.

21. **brave**   Lifesavers are brave people.

22. **having**   We were having a good time.

23. **centre**   A bee is in the centre of a flower.

24. **slice**   He ate a slice of bread.

25. **outside**   We play outside in fine weather.

26. **walked**   They walked to the supermarket.

27. **smiling**   The happy crowd was smiling.

28. **worker**   That busy man is a good worker.

29. **clown**   The clown was very funny.

30. **twenty**   Ten plus ten equals twenty.

31. **chairs**   We sat down on our chairs.

32. **wonderful** The party was wonderful.

33. **teacher**   My teacher helps me to learn.

34. **clear**   The clear sky had no clouds.

35. **follow**   Please follow your leader.

36. **cried**   Baby cried as he was hungry.

37. **idea**   That's a good idea! Let's do it.

38. **float**   My ball can float on the water.

39. **mountain** We looked up at a mountain.

40. **stories**   Bedtime stories are great.

Mark   / 20   Mark   / 20

Checklist

The student has demonstrated the ability to ...

- ○ understand and apply both long and short sounds when reading, spelling and writing
- ○ recognise word families where words rhyme and have a common base
- ○ understand that not all words with the same base rhyme (eg save/have; but/put)
- ○ understand that some letters have a different sound in different words (eg **g** sound in 'goat' and 'giraffe'; **c** sound in 'comic' and 'cents')
- ○ recognise and apply common blends – bl, pl, st, dr   etc
- ○ recognise and apply special blends – th, sh, wh , ch in word families and core words
- ○ understand and use syllables to decipher words
- ○ build on word families to extend beyond the examples given, using their Personal Word Box
- ○ recognise sight words and use phonic clues to help decipher them
- ○ read simple compound words and create some of their own using known words in word families
- ○ break compound words into the separate words it contains
- ○ understand and apply word endings (eg s, es, d, ed, ing, er as appropriate)
- ○ apply specific spelling rules with relevant activities provided in context
- ○ recognise homographs (eg bank/bank) and homophones (eg one/won)
- ○ recognise palindromes and have fun doing thematic word puzzles
- ○ successfully complete a wide range of graded activities designed to assist understanding and application of phonics when reading, spelling and writing
- ○ score well in the assessment tasks provided

Teacher Comment: